CONTENTS

INTRODUCTION

I was able to lose 80 pounds in 2009 and keep them off by eating only regular everyday Superfoods. After several Superfoods related books, I decided to write one about smoothies for diabetics. I hope you will enjoy the recipes I prepared for you. Recipes have only ingredients listed and instructions how to blend a perfect smoothie are given here as a short introduction:

Put the liquid in first. Surrounded by tea or yogurt, the blender blades can move freely. Next, add chunks of fruits or vegetables. Leafy greens are going into the pitcher last. Preferred liquid is green tea, but you can use almond or coconut milk or herbal tea.

Start slow. If your blender has speeds, start it on low to break up big pieces of fruit. Continue blending until you get a puree. If your blender can pulse, pulse a few times before switching to a puree mode. Once you have your liquid and fruit pureed, start adding greens, very slowly. Wait until previous batch of greens has been completely blended. I use <u>Vitamix</u> blenders because they're sturdy and offer 7 year warranty. That was definitely the best investment in my health.

Thicken? Added too much tea or coconut milk? Thicken your smoothie by adding ice cubes, flax meal, chia seeds or oatmeal. Once you get used to various tastes of smoothies, add any seaweed, spirulina, chlorella powder or ginger for additional kick. Experiment with any Superfoods in powder form at this point. Think of adding any nut butter or sesame paste too or some Superfoods oils.

Rotate! Rotate your greens; don't always drink the same smoothie! At the beginning try 2 different greens every week and later introduce third and fourth one weekly. And keep rotating them. Don't use spinach and kale all the time. Try beets greens, they have a pinch of pink in them and that add great color to your smoothie. Here is the list of leafy green for you to try: spinach, kale, dandelion, chards, beet leaves, arugula, lettuce, collard greens, bok choy, cabbage, cilantro, parsley.

Flavor! Flavor smoothies with ground vanilla bean, cinnamon, ½ tsp. of lucuma powder, nutmeg, cloves, almond butter, cayenne pepper, ginger or just about any seeds or chopped nuts combination.

Not only are green smoothies high in nutrients, vitamins and fiber, they can also make any vegetable you probably don't like (be it kale, spinach or broccoli) taste great. The secret behind blending the perfect smoothie is using sweet fruits or nuts or seeds to give your drink a unique taste.

There's a reason kale and spinach seem to be the main ingredients in almost every green smoothie. Not only do they give smoothies their verdant color, they are also packed with calcium, protein and iron. Although blending alone increases the accessibility of carotenoids, since the presence of fats is known to increase carotenoid absorption from leafy greens, it is possible that coconut oil, nuts and seeds in a smoothie could increase absorption further.

Fruits and Veggies preparation

• Wash fruits and veggies

• Pluck leaves and stems from berries

• Core apples (optional)

• Peel orange, lemon, lime, grapefruit, kiwi, beet, pomegranate, ginger, dragon fruit and banana

• Peel and take the seeds out of papaya

• Remove seeds from peppers, apricots, peaches, cherries, plums and prunes

• Mangos, melons and avocados should be peeled, and inner seed taken out

• Watermelons should have their outer rind removed.

• Scoop out the flesh from passion fruit

• Cut fruits and veggies in 2-inch slices

If you can't find some ingredient, replace it with the closest one.

RED SMOOTHIES

Carrot Date Smoothie

---

2 Carrots

2 Apples

1 cup of crushed ice

Pinch of nutmeg

½ tsp. Cinnamon

1 tbsp. Minced ginger

Spinach Berries Smoothie

- ½ cup almond milk

- ½ cup water

- 1 carrot

- 1 cup spinach

- 1 cup frozen raspberries

- 1 tablespoon <u>Chia</u> seeds

- 1 tablespoon fresh mint

- ½ teaspoon <u>Lucuma</u> powder

Strawberry Carrot Smoothie

- 1 cup frozen strawberries

- 1 banana

- 1 carrot

- 1 cup crushed ice

- 2 tablespoons <u>Hemp</u> seeds

- 1 tsp. Fresh Mint

Red Peppers Tomato Salad Smoothie

1 cup Red Peppers

1/2 medium avocado

2 medium tomatoes

1 cucumber

2 tablespoons lemon juice

1 tsp. olive oil & 1 tsp. chopped garlic

Pinch of sea salt & 1 tbsp. dill

1/2 cup crushed ice

Apricots & Carrots Smoothie

4 apricots

1 apple

1 cup red spinach

2 carrots

1 cup water

1 tbsp. <u>Maca</u>

Strawberries Yogurt Smoothie

- 1 cup strawberries

- ½ cup low-fat plain yogurt

- 3 ice cubes

- 1 tbsp. Ground coconut

- 1 tbsp. <u>Acai</u>

Red Swiss Smoothie

- 1 cup Red Swiss chard
- ½ cup raspberries, frozen
- 1/2 cup peaches, frozen
- 1 tbsp. Pumpkin seeds
- 1 orange
- 1 cup crushed ice

Red Leaf Lettuce Smoothie

- 1 cup Red Leaf Lettuce

- 1 Bananas

- 1 Celery stalk

- 1/2 cup Strawberry

- 1/2 cup Raspberry

- 1 cup crushed ice

- 1 clove & pinch of nutmeg

Red Veggie Smoothie

- 1 cup chopped tomato

- 1 kiwi

- 1 banana

- 1/2 celery stalk

- 1/4 cup each cilantro and spinach

- 1 tbsp. Olive oil

- Pinch of sea salt

- 1/2 cup ice

Papaya Diva Smoothie

- 1 cup Red Endive

- 1 cup chopped Papaya

- 1 banana

- 1 tbsp. chopped fresh Ginger

- 1 cup crushed ice

- 1 tbsp. Cashew butter

- Top with <u>Goji berries</u>

Tomato Onion Smoothie

- 2 Tomatoes
- 1/2 Cucumber
- ¼ cup Cilantro
- 1/2 of small onion
- 1 tbsp. Olive oil
- 1 cup crushed ice
- Juice of 1/2 lime
- 1 Avocado
- Pinch of sea salt
- 1 tbsp. Fresh Basil

Pomegranates & Berries smoothie

- 1 cup Cherries

- ½ cup Raspberries

- 1 cup Pomegranates

- ½ cup Strawberries

- 1 cup <u>Yerba</u> Mate tea

- 1 tbsp. <u>Chlorella</u>

Swiss Peach Smoothie

- 1 cup Red Swiss chard

- ½ cup raspberries, frozen

- 1/2 cup peaches, frozen

- 1 blood orange

- 1 cup crushed ice

- 1 tbsp. <u>Maca</u>

- 1 tbsp. Coconut flakes on top

Avocado Carrot Smoothie

- 2 carrots

- 1 banana

- ½ avocado

- 2 apple

- Juice of ½ lemon

- 1 cup crushed ice

- 1 tsp. ginger

- Top with ½ tsp. <u>Bee Pollen</u>

Radicchio Cranberry Smoothie

- 1 cup fresh Cranberries

- 1 apple

- ½ cup Red Spinach

- ½ Avocado

- 1/2 cup chopped Radicchio

- 1 tbsp. <u>Acai</u>

- 1 cup crushed ice

Red Currants Pumpkin Smoothie

- 1 cup pumpkin puree

- 1 cup red currants

- 1 cup ginger tea

- 1/2 tsp. <u>Lucuma</u> powder

- 1 clove

- Pinch of nutmeg

- Pinch of cinnamon

- 1 tbsp. <u>Chia</u> Seeds

Cucumber Beet Smoothie

- 1 Large Beet

- ½ Cucumber

- 1 Apple

- 1 clove garlic

- 1 tbsp. Minced ginger

- 1 cup crushed ice

- 1 tbsp. Crushed Seaweed (Wakame or Arame)

Rhubarb Avocado Smoothie

- 1 cup chopped Rhubarb

- 1/2 Avocado

- 1 cup hibiscus tea

- 1 tbsp. Cacao nibs

- 1 tbsp. Chopped pecans

- 2 tbsp. Sesame seeds sprinkled

Blood Orange Smoothie

- 2 Blood Oranges

- 2 carrots

- 1 cup Raspberries

- 1 cup hibiscus tea

- 1 tbsp. Walnuts

- 2 tbsp. Ground <u>flax</u> seeds

Papaya Red Spinach Smoothie

- 1 cup chopped Papaya

- 1 banana

- 1 cup red spinach

- 1 cup crushed ice

- 1 tablespoon <u>Maca</u>

- Top with 1 tablespoon dried chokecherries

Red Grapefruit Smoothie

- 1 large red Grapefruit

- 1 cup Red Endive

- 1 cup crushed ice

- 2 tbsp. Sunflower seeds butter

- 1 tbsp. <u>Hemp</u> seeds sprinkled

Raspberry Red Lettuce Smoothie

- 1 cup Red Leaf Lettuce

- 1 cup frozen Raspberries

- 2 Red Apples

- 1 tbsp. <u>Goji berries</u>

- 1 cup white tea

Cranberry Red Leaf Lettuce Smoothie

- 1 cups Red Leaf Lettuce

- 1 Banana

- 1 tbsp. Tahini

- 1 cup fresh Cranberries

- 1 cup crushed ice

- Top with Coconut flakes

PURPLE SMOOTHIES

Red Dragon Fruit (Pitaya) Smoothie

- 2 purple carrots

- 2 tbsp. Almond Butter

- 1 cup Red Dragon fruit (Pitaya)

- 1 tbsp. Maca

- 1 Blood Orange

- 1 cup crushed ice

Blueberry Yogurt & Spinach Smoothie

- 1 cup blueberries

- 1 avocado

- 1 cup Red Chard

- 1 cup Yogurt

- 1/2 cup Mulberry

- 1 tbsp. Ground <u>flax</u> seeds

- ½ tsp. Cinnamon

- Top with Blueberries and Coconut flakes

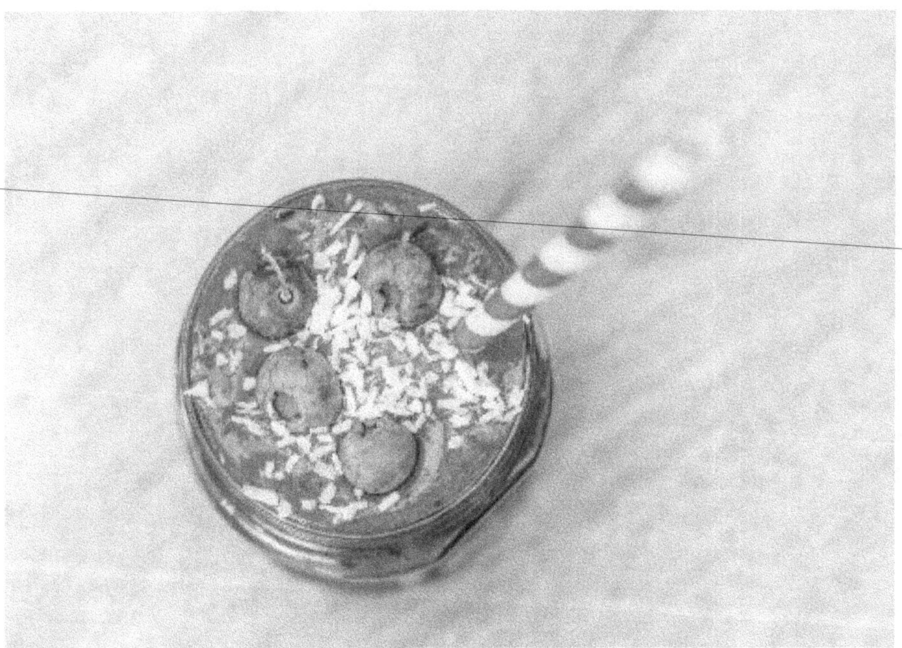

Beet Apple Smoothie

- 1 cup crushed ice
- 1/2 avocado, pitted
- 1 cup frozen strawberries
- 1 lemon, juiced
- 2 chopped celery stalks
- 1 large beet
- 1 apple
- 1 tablespoon <u>coconut</u> oil
- 1 tbsp. <u>Acai</u>

Blueberry Avocado Smoothie

- 1/2 avocado

- 1 cup spinach

- 1 cup blueberries, frozen

- 1 tsp. <u>coconut</u> oil

- 3/4 cup water

- 1 cup crushed ice

- Top with Cranberries

Beet & Beet Smoothie

- 2 cups Beet Greens

- 1 cup crushed ice

- 2 blood oranges,

- 1 large Beet root

- Juice of ½ lemon

- 1 tbsp. <u>Hemp</u> seeds

Chokecherry Cauliflower Smoothie

- 1 cup Chokecherries or 1/2 cup of dried Chokecherries

- ½ cup cauliflower

- 1 cup kefir

- 3 ice cubes

- 1 tbsp. <u>Matcha</u>

Purple Beet Smoothie

- 2 large beets

- ½ Avocado

- 1 cup Raspberry

- 1 tbsp. <u>Chia</u> seeds

- 1 carrot

- 1 cup crushed ice

Purple Cabbage smoothie

- 1 cup Red Cabbage

- ½ Avocado

- 1 Kiwi

- 1 Banana

- 1 Brazil Nut

- 1 cup hibiscus tea

- 1 tbsp. Spirulina

- 1 cup crushed ice

Purple Cauliflower Smoothie

- 1 cup Purple cauliflower

- 1 banana

- 1 cup Black Currants

- 1 tbsp. <u>Chlorella</u>

- 1 cup Chai tea

Acai Strawberries Smoothie

- 1 cup Acai berries or 1/4 cup of <u>Acai</u> powder

- ½ cup strawberries

- 1 cup low-fat plain yogurt

- 3 ice cubes

- 1/2 tsp. <u>Bee Pollen</u>

Red Grapefruit & Beets Smoothie

- 1 Red Grapefruit

- 1 large beet

- 1/2 cup frozen sliced peaches

- 1/2 cup frozen strawberries

- 1 tbsp. <u>Maca</u>

- 1 cup crushed ice

Purple Carrots Smoothie

- 3 purple carrots

- 2 tbsp. Almond Butter

- 1 cup Blackberries

- 1 tbsp. <u>Chlorella</u>

- 1 Orange

- 1 cup crushed ice

Blueberry Banana Smoothie

- 1 cup Blueberries

- 1 apple

- 1 banana

- 1 cup Red endive

- ½ cup crushed ice

- ½ cup water

- Top with <u>Goji berries</u> and shredded coconut

Beet Kale Smoothie

- 1 large beet
- 1 apple
- 1 blood orange
- ½ cup frozen blackberries
- 1 cup kale
- ½ cup crushed ice
- ½ cup water
- 1 tbsp. <u>Hemp</u> Seeds

Purple Kale Smoothie

- 1 cup Purple Kale

- 2 apples

- Ginger

- 1 Banana

- 1 cup frozen Blueberries

- 2 tbsp. _Spirulina_

- 1 cup Green tea

Purple Queen Smoothie

- 2 purple carrots

- 2 tbsp. Almond Butter

- 1 cup Red Dragon fruit (Pitaya)

- 1 tbsp. <u>Maca</u>

- 1 blood Orange

- 1 cup crushed ice

Black Smoothie

- 2 cups spinach

- 1 cup low fat plain yogurt

- 1 banana

- 1/2 cup blueberries, frozen

- 1 cup blackberries, frozen

- 1 tbsp. Cashew nuts

- 1 cup crushed ice

Blueberry Kefir & Spinach Smoothie

- 1 cup blueberries

- 1 cup chopped Cantaloupe

- 1 cup Red Spinach

- 1 cup Green tea

- 1 tbsp. <u>Hemp</u> seeds

- ½ tsp. Cinnamon

GREEN SMOOTHIES

Kale Kiwi Smoothie

- 1 cup Kale, chopped

- 2 Apples

- 3 Kiwis

- 1 tablespoon <u>flax</u> seed

- 1/2 tsp. royal jelly

- 1 cup crushed ice

Zucchini Apples Smoothie

- 1/2 cup zucchini

- 2 Apples

- 3/4 avocado

- 1 stalk Celery

- 1 Lemon

- 1 tbsp. Spirulina

- 1 1/2 cups crushed ice

Dandelion Smoothie

- 1 cup Dandelion greens

- 1 cup Spinach

- ½ cup tahini

- 1 Red Radish

- 1 tbsp. <u>Chia</u> seeds

- 1 cup lavender tea

Broccoli Apple Smoothie

- 1 Apple
- 1 cup Broccoli
- 1 tbsp. Cilantro
- 1 Celery stalk
- 1 cup crushed ice
- 1 tbsp. crushed Seaweed

Salad Smoothie

- 1 cup spinach
- ½ cucumber
- 1/2 small onion
- 2 tablespoons Parsley
- 2 tablespoons lemon juice
- 1 cup crushed ice
- 1 tbsp. olive oil
- ¼ cup Wheatgrass

Avocado Kale Smoothie

- 1 cup Kale

- ½ Avocado

- 1 cup Cucumber

- 1 Celery Stalk

- 1 tbsp. <u>Chia</u> seeds

- 1 cup chamomile tea

- 1 tbsp. <u>Spirulina</u>

Watercress Smoothie

- 1 cup Watercress

- ½ cup almond butter

- 2 small cucumbers

- 1 cup coconut milk

- 1 tbsp. <u>Chlorella</u>

- 1 tbsp. <u>Black cumin</u>– sprinkle on top and garnish with parsley

Beet Greens Smoothie

- 1 cup Beet Greens

- 2 tbsp. Pumpkin seeds butter

- 1 cup Strawberry

- 1 tbsp. Sesame seeds

- 1 tbsp. <u>Hemp</u> seeds

- 1 cup chamomile tea

Broccoli Leeks Cucumber smoothie

- 1 cup Broccoli

- 2 tbsp. Cashew butter

- 2 Leeks

- 2 Cucumbers

- 1 Lime

- ½ cup Lettuce

- ½ cup Leaf Lettuce

- 1 tbsp. <u>Matcha</u>

- 1 cup crushed ice

Cacao Spinach Smoothie

- 2 cups spinach

- 1 cup blueberries, frozen

- 1 tablespoons dark cocoa powder

- ½ cup unsweetened almond milk

- 1/2 cup crushed ice

- 1/2 tsp Lucuma powder

- 1 tbsp. Matcha powder

Flax Almond Butter Smoothie

- ½ cup plain yogurt

- 2 tablespoons almond butter

- 2 cups spinach

- 1 banana, frozen

- 3 strawberries

- 1/2 cup crushed ice

- 1 teaspoon <u>flax</u> seed

Apple Kale Smoothie

- 1 cup kale

- ½ cup coconut milk

- 1 tbsp. <u>Maca</u>

- 1 banana, frozen

- ¼ teaspoon cinnamon

- 1 Apple

- Pinch of nutmeg

- 1 clove

- 3 ice cubes

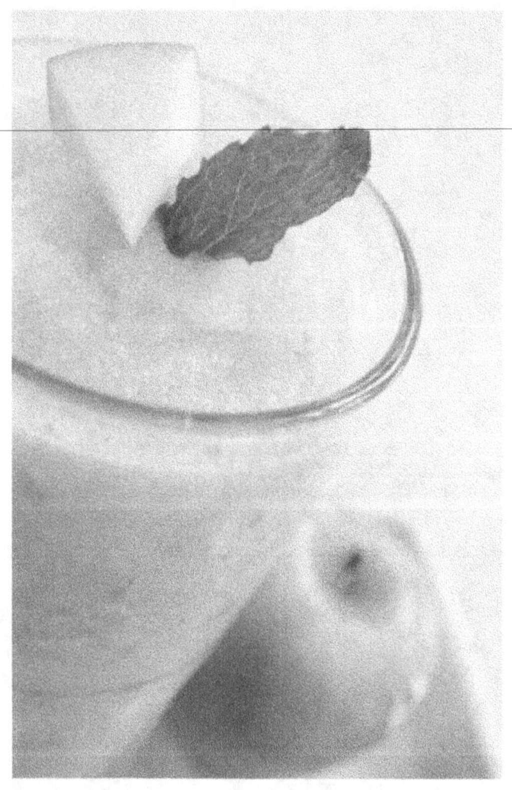

Iceberg Peach Smoothie

- 1 cup Iceberg lettuce

- 1 Banana

- 1 small peach

- 1 Brazil Nut

- 1 small Mango

- 1 cup Kombucha

- Top with <u>Hemp</u> seeds

Kiwi Apple & Leaf Lettuce Smoothie

- 1 cup Leaf Lettuce

- 2 Apples

- 2 kiwis

- 1/4 Lemon

- 1 tbsp. <u>Chlorella</u>

- 1 cup crushed ice

Banana Spinach Raspberry Smoothie

- 1 cup Spinach

- 2 Bananas

- 2 <u>dates</u>

- ½ cup Raspberries

- 1 tbsp. Ground <u>flax</u> seeds

- 1 cup crushed ice

- 1 tbsp. Cilantro

Endive Apples Smoothie

- 1 cup Endive
- 2 Apples
- 1 Tbsp. Dill
- 1 stalk Celery
- 1/2 Lemon
- 1 tbsp. Matcha
- 1 cup crushed ice

Spinach Celery Parsley Smoothie

- 1 cup Spinach

- 1 Peach

- 1 avocado

- 2 stalks Celery

- 1 Lime

- 1 tbsp. <u>Chia</u> seeds

- 1 cup crushed ice

- 1 tbsp. Parsley

Swiss chard Cucumber Celery Carrot Smoothie

- 1 cup Swiss chard
- 2 Carrots
- 1 Cucumber
- 2 stalks Celery
- 1 Tbsp. <u>Lucuma</u> powder
- 1 tbsp. Parsley
- 1 cup crushed ice

Kale Cucumber Lime Apples Smoothie

- 1 cup Kale

- 2 Apples

- 1 avocado

- 1 Lime

- 1/4 cup Raspberries

- 1 Cucumber

- 1 cup crushed ice

Kiwi Zucchini Smoothie

- 1 cup zucchini

- 2 Apples

- 1/2 avocado

- 3 kiwis

- 1 tbsp. _Spirulina_

- 1 cup crushed ice

Avocado Kale Smoothie

- 1 cup Kale

- 1 Apple

- 2 avocados

- 1 stalk Celery

- 1/2 Lime

- 1 tbsp. Cilantro

- 1 cup crushed ice

Flax Kiwi Spinach Smoothie

- 1 cup Spinach

- 2 Apples

- 1 banana

- 1 stalk Celery

- 3 Kiwis

- 3 tbsp. ground <u>flax</u> seeds

- 1 cup crushed ice

Parsley Arugula Cucumber Apples Smoothie

- 1 cup Arugula
- 1 Cucumber
- 2 apples
- 1 stalk Celery
- 1 tbsp. Parsley
- 1 cup crushed ice

Celery Cucumber Cabbage Apples Smoothie

- 1/2 cup shredded cabbage

- 1 Apple

- 1 avocado

- 2 stalks Celery

- 1 Lemon

- 1 Zucchini

- 1 cup crushed ice

Kale Banana Apples Smoothie

- 1 cup Kale

- 2 Apples

- 3/4 avocado

- 1 banana

- 1 tbsp. <u>Maqui</u>

- 1 cup crushed ice

Zucchini Celery Apples Smoothie

- 1 zucchini

- 2 Apples

- 3/4 avocado

- 2 stalk Celery

- 1 jalapeno pepper

- 1 cup crushed ice

Leaf Lettuce Apples Spinach Smoothie

- 1/2 cup Spinach

- 2 Apples

- 2 Tbsp. almond butter

- 1 cup Leaf Lettuce

- 1/2 Lemon

- 1 tbsp. Chlorella

- 1 cup crushed ice

Zucchini Parsley Smoothie

- 1 zucchini

- 2 Apples

- ½ cup Parsley

- 1 stalk Celery

- ½ Lime

- 1 tbsp. Sesame seeds

- 1 cup crushed ice

Dandelion Banana Smoothie

- 1 cup Dandelion leaves

- 2 Bananas

- 3/4 avocado

- 1 Orange

- 1 tbsp. <u>Spirulina</u>

- 1 cup crushed ice

Leaf Lettuce Parsley Smoothie

- 1/2 cup Parsley

- 2 Apples

- 1 cup Leaf Lettuce

- 2 Tbsp. Sunflower butter

- 1 Yellow Grapefruit

- 1 tbsp. <u>Hemp</u> Hearts

- 1 cup crushed ice

Chia Apples Spinach Smoothie

- 1 cup Spinach or mustard greens

- 2 Apples

- 2 tbsp. Tahini

- 3 tbsp. Chia seeds

- 1 cup crushed ice

Grapefruit Kale Watercress Smoothie

- 1 large grapefruit

- 1 Apple

- 1 cup watercress

- 2 Kale leaves

- 1 Tbsp. dill (optional)

- 1 cup crushed ice

Collard Greens Parsley and Banana Smoothie

- 1 cup chopped collard greens

- 2 bananas

- 1 Tbsp. chopped parsley

- 1 tbsp. <u>Chlorella</u>

- 1 cup crushed ice

Dandelion Apples Smoothie

- 1 cup Dandelion leaves

- 1 orange

- 3/4 avocado

- 1 stalk Celery or 1 broccoli floret

- 1 tsp. chopped fresh ginger

- 1 cup crushed ice

WHITE SMOOTHIES

White Cauliflower Smoothie

• 1 cup Kefir

• 1 cup White cauliflower florets

• 1 fig

• Juice of ½ lemon

• 1/2 cup crushed ice

• 1 tbsp. Minced ginger

• 1 tbsp. Maca

• few Hazelnuts

Coconut Chia Pudding

- 1/4 cup <u>Chia</u> seeds

- 1 cup coconut milk

- 1/2 tablespoon Royall jelly

- 1 tsp. Ground <u>Vanilla</u> Bean

- a pinch of Nutmeg

- Top with Blueberries

White Kefir Smoothie

- ½ cup plain kefir

- 1 banana

- 1 tablespoon sunflower butter

- 1 tbsp. <u>Maca</u>

- ½ tsp. Cinnamon

- Top with Apple slices, cherries and lime

Tzataziki Smoothie

- 1 cup kefir or plain Greek yogurt

- 1 cucumber

- 1 avocado

- 1 tbsp. Fresh dill or mint

- 1 tablespoon lemon juice

- 1 teaspoon sea salt

- 1 teaspoon Sesame seeds

Coconut Smoothie

- 1 cup of Coconut Milk

- 1 banana

- 1 White Peach

- 1 tablespoon tahini

- 1 tbsp. _Hemp_ seeds

- a pinch of Nutmeg

- Top with Coconut flakes

Cacao Blackberries Chia Pudding

- 1/4 cup <u>Chia</u> seeds

- 1 cup coconut milk

- 1/2 tsp. <u>Lucuma</u>

- 1 tbsp. <u>Maca</u>

- Top with Blackberries

Coconut Yogurt Smoothie

- 1 Cup of low fat Greek Yogurt

- 1 banana

- 1 tablespoon Coconut flakes

- 1 tablespoon <u>Hemp</u> seeds

- Top with whipped Coconut Cream

Coconut Pomegranate Chia Pudding

- 1/4 cup <u>Chia</u> seeds

- 1 cup Coconut milk

- 1/2 tsp <u>Lucuma</u> powder

- 1/2 tablespoon Coconut flakes

- Top with Pomegranate seeds

Yellow Smoothies

Cauliflower Smoothie

- 1 cup White cauliflower florets

- 1 small Mango

- 1 passion fruit

- 1/2 tsp. <u>Bee Pollen</u>

- 1 cup crushed ice

- Pinch of nutmeg

Papaya Smoothie

- 1 banana

- 1 cup spinach

- 1 cup chopped papaya

- 1 cup crushed ice

- 1 tbsp. <u>Chia</u> seeds

Swiss Papaya Smoothie

- 1 Papaya

- 1 Banana

- 1 cup Swiss chard

- 1 cup Lemongrass tea

- 1 tbsp. <u>Matcha</u>

Pumpkin Banana Smoothie

- 1 cup pumpkin puree

- 1 banana

- 1 cup ginger tea

- 1/2 tsp. <u>Lucuma</u> powder

- 1 clove

- Pinch of nutmeg

- Pinch of cinnamon

- Top with <u>Hemp</u> seeds

RAINBOW SMOOTHIE

3 Colors Rainbow Smoothie

• Blend 1 Large beet with some crushed ice

• Blend 3 carrots with some crashed ice

• Blend 1 cucumber, 1 cup of leaf lettuce, some ice and ½ cup Wheatgrass

• Serve them separate to preserve the distinct color